CAREER FINDER

WORK IN THE FASHION INDUSTRY

by Emma Huddleston

BrightPoint Press

San Diego, CA

BrightPoint Press

© 2020 BrightPoint Press
an imprint of ReferencePoint Press, Inc.
Printed in the United States

For more information, contact:
BrightPoint Press
PO Box 27779
San Diego, CA 92198
www.BrightPointPress.com

ALL RIGHTS RESERVED.
No part of this work covered by the copyright hereon may be reproduced or used in any form or by any means—graphic, electronic, or mechanical, including photocopying, recording, taping, web distribution, or information storage retrieval systems—without the written permission of the publisher.

LIBRARY OF CONGRESS CATALOGING-IN-PUBLICATION DATA

Names: Huddleston, Emma, author.
Title: Work in the fashion industry / by Emma Huddleston.
Description: San Diego, CA : ReferencePoint Press, Inc., 2020. | Series: Career finder | Includes index. | Audience: Grades 9 to 12.
Identifiers: LCCN 2019003310 (print) | LCCN 2019003558 (ebook) | ISBN 9781682827260 (ebook) | ISBN 9781682827253 (hardcover)
Subjects: LCSH: Fashion--Vocational guidance--Juvenile literature. | Clothing trade--Vocational guidance--Juvenile literature.
Classification: LCC TT507 (ebook) | LCC TT507 .H75 2020 (print) | DDC 746.9/2023--dc23
LC record available at https://lccn.loc.gov/2019003310

CONTENTS

THE FASHION INDUSTRY   4

INTRODUCTION   6
    WHAT IS THE FASHION INDUSTRY?

CHAPTER ONE   12
    DESIGNER

CHAPTER TWO   26
    MODEL

CHAPTER THREE   42
    ART DIRECTOR

CHAPTER FOUR   52
    MARKET RESEARCHER

CHAPTER FIVE   64
    RETAIL SALESPERSON

Interview with a Professional   74
Other Jobs in the Fashion Industry   76
Glossary   77
Index   78
Image Credits   79
About the Author   80

THE FASHION INDUSTRY

Fashion Designers

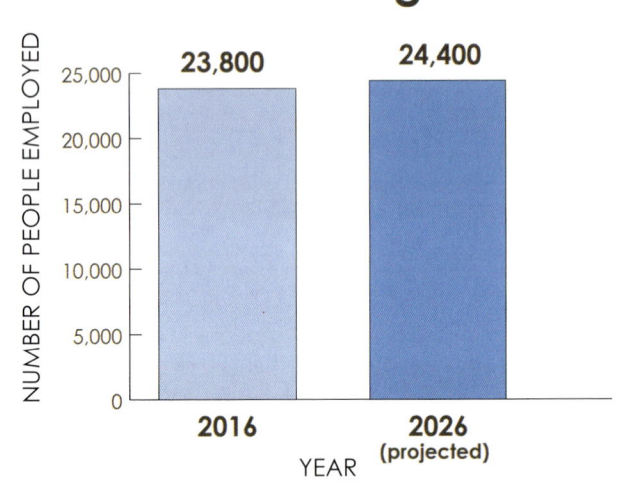

YEAR	NUMBER OF PEOPLE EMPLOYED
2016	23,800
2026 (projected)	24,400

Art Directors

YEAR	NUMBER OF PEOPLE EMPLOYED
2016	90,300
2026 (projected)	95,200

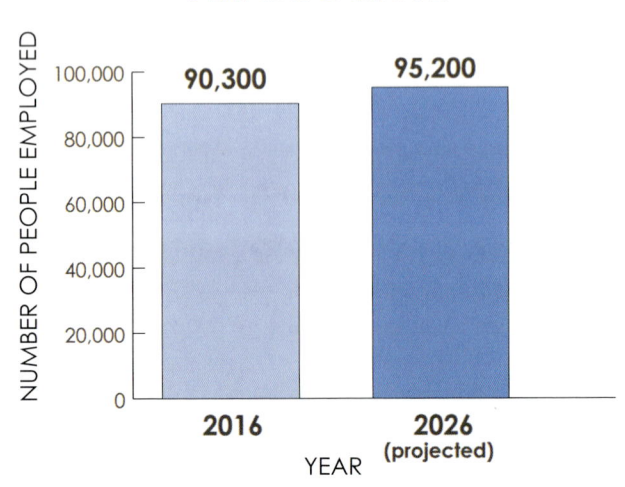

Value of the Fashion Industry (in Billions)

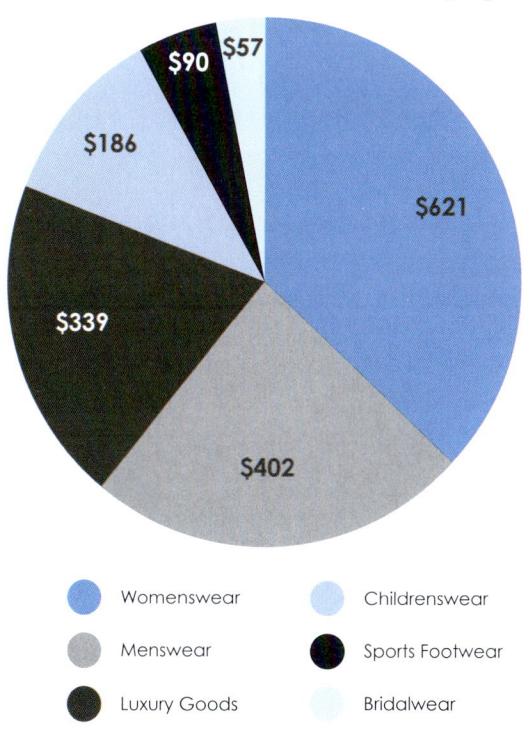

- Womenswear: $621
- Menswear: $402
- Luxury Goods: $339
- Childrenswear: $186
- Sports Footwear: $90
- Bridalwear: $57

INTRODUCTION

WHAT IS THE FASHION INDUSTRY?

Cameras flash. Models strut down a **runway**. The mall is having a fashion show. People stop shopping to watch. The models wear new clothing. Designers made this clothing. It is fashionable. It has stylish patterns and designs.

Many people work together to put on a fashion show.

Photographers surround the runway. They take photographs of the models. Their photos may appear on news sites or fashion blogs. Some photos may be featured in magazines. Many people look at fashion sites and magazines. They learn the latest styles. This can influence the clothes they buy. They may buy new clothes in retail stores. Then stores gain more customers.

Inside stores, salespeople dress mannequins in the latest styles. Mannequins are life-size figures that look like people. Some are displayed near store windows. These displays attract people who pass by. Customers can see how the clothes may look on them.

Models, photographers, and salespeople are all part of the fashion industry. Fashion

Photographers capture the looks and styles of models at fashion shows.

is a part of daily life. People wear coats when it is cold. They put on tennis shoes for walking long distances. People need different clothes for all types of activities.

Designers create clothing that is fashionable and comfortable.

Fashion also shows off style and personality. Designers create unique looks. Many different people work in the fashion industry. Some jobs are creative.

Some people make and design products. Others work on the business side. They buy products and sell them to stores. Salespeople in stores sell the products to customers.

Promoting the products is an important job. People who work in the media spread news about fashion. They tell the public about new trends. Models and photographers show off products.

The fashion industry is always growing and changing. New fashion trends are made each year. There are job opportunities for all kinds of people.

CHAPTER ONE

DESIGNER

Designers are at the core of the fashion industry. They make ideas come to life. They design clothing, jewelry, and accessories. Models, companies, and **consumers** use products made by designers. Designers make items that people use every day. They give products style and personality.

MINIMUM EDUCATION: Bachelor's degree

PERSONAL QUALITIES: Artistic, creative, detail-oriented, a good communicator, knowledgeable about computers

CERTIFICATION AND LICENSING: None

WORKING CONDITIONS: Many designers work for companies. Others are self-employed.

SALARY: The average **salary** in 2017 was $67,420 per year, or $32.41 per hour. The lowest 10 percent earned less than $33,910 per year. The highest 10 percent earned more than $135,490 per year.

NUMBER OF JOBS: 23,800 in 2016

FUTURE JOB OUTLOOK: The number of jobs is expected to grow 3% from 2016 to 2026, or an additional 600 jobs.

WHAT THEY DO

Designers create original products. First they come up with an idea for a product.

Designers create unique fashions and styles.

They could be inspired by another person's clothing. Or they may make a product that looks like a plant or an animal.

Next, designers sketch their designs. Some use paper and colored pencils.

Others use computers. Computer-aided design (CAD) involves using computer programs. It helps designers see a model of their product. They can experiment with sizes and shapes. They can view different colors or patterns.

Designers select materials. Clothing designers choose fabric and patterns. They might want specific colors. They choose fabric that is comfortable. A thick fabric is better for outdoor clothing. It is strong and warm. Thin fabric is better for layering.

Designers create unique styles. Their styles reflect their personalities and tastes.

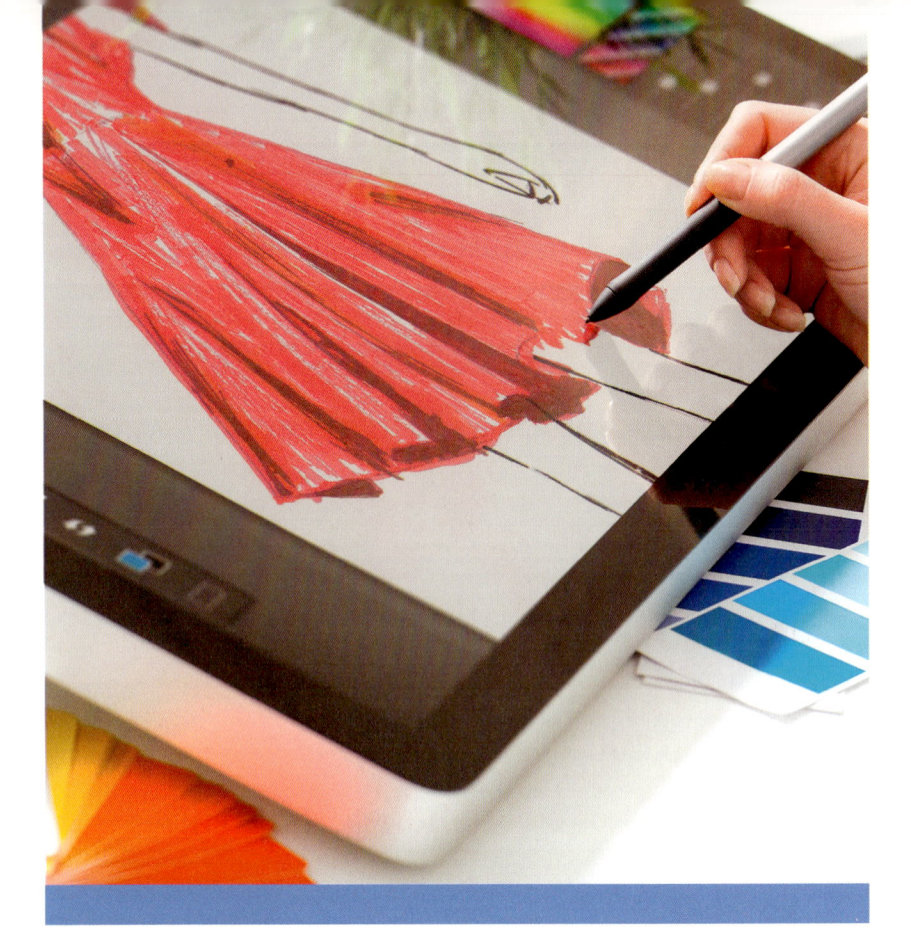

Some designers use special programs to create their designs.

Nicole Miller is an American fashion designer. She has designed furniture and other home products. She also started her own clothing line. She mainly designs women's clothing. She said, "I want women to feel confident when they are wearing my clothing. I think the most important thing . . . is that clothes should give you confidence."

Different products require different materials. Jewelry designers may choose beads, chains, or jewels. Designers like to touch and feel each material. It helps them decide which materials will make their designs come to life. Tom Ford is a designer. He said, "I take every opportunity to learn what I can in terms of quality of ingredients, or inspiration to make people dream." He aims to inspire people with his designs.

Designer Nicole Miller greets the crowd at one of her fashion shows.

A designer's next step is to create the product. Some designers make the first version by hand. They work with the materials to get it just right. Other designers tell other people how to make the product.

The designer gives them feedback until the product looks the way the designer wants.

Finally, designers show their products to buyers. Buyers work for clothing companies or other fashion-related companies. They may purchase the products. Then the products are sold in stores. People can buy them in stores or on store websites.

Sometimes designers travel to trade shows. A trade show is an event for professionals in the industry. Designers show off their work at trade shows. They see other designers' work. They look at different fabrics. They learn about new fashion trends. This might inspire them to create a new product.

TRAINING

Most designers get a bachelor's degree. They specialize in fashion design or a similar **major**. In school, they learn CAD. They study different materials and fabrics. They create a portfolio. A portfolio is a collection of design ideas and projects. It shows what a designer has created. Designers show their portfolios to employers to get a job.

Designers often work as assistant designers at first. They get experience working with another designer. They see

Some designers create products for the home, such as bedding. They can learn about popular styles at trade shows.

how the industry works before working independently. They try designing different products. Some designers choose to specialize in one area of fashion.

There are four main types of designers. They are clothing, footwear, accessory, and costume designers. Some clothing

Two or more designers sometimes work together on a project.

designers create clothes for all people. Others specialize in creating clothing for one group. They might design clothing for children or athletes. Or they might design clothing for formal events. Some people design footwear, such as hiking boots or sandals. Accessory designers create products ranging from glasses to purses to hats. Costume designers work with theater, television, and movie companies. They design costumes for actors.

LOOKING AHEAD

Being a designer takes perseverance. Designers sometimes work long hours before fashion shows. Some work as assistants for years before they become successful enough to work on their own.

Some designers create historical costumes. They research a time period to learn about the fashions that were popular.

Careers in fashion design are competitive. Many creative people are drawn to this job. Designing fashion is exciting. Designers are always in demand.

FIND OUT MORE

The Arts Schools Network

website: www.artsschoolsnetwork.org

The Arts Schools Network connects leaders in art and design to students and organizations.

The Council of Fashion Designers of America, Inc. (CFDA)

website: www.cfda.com

The CFDA promotes American fashion around the world. More than 500 American designers are members of the CFDA.

The National Association of Schools of Art and Design (NASAD)

website: https://nasad.arts-accredit.org

NASAD aims to help students and professionals in the art and design field. It offers educational resources and programs.

CHAPTER TWO

MODEL

Models are the face of the fashion industry. They show off fashion products. They appear in ads. They model products at fashion shows. Their job is to help sell fashion.

WHAT THEY DO

Models promote products. They do this in several ways. Some appear in commercials for stores that sell fashion products. They

MINIMUM EDUCATION: None

PERSONAL QUALITIES: Disciplined, organized, persistent, competitive, a good listener, stylish

CERTIFICATION AND LICENSING: None

WORKING CONDITIONS: The workplace varies. Many models work in indoor studios or on runways.

SALARY: The average salary in 2017 was $22,900 per year, or $11.01 per hour. The lowest 10 percent earned less than $8.17 per hour. The highest 10 percent earned more than $23.78 per hour.

NUMBER OF JOBS: 4,800 in 2016

FUTURE JOB OUTLOOK: The number of jobs is not expected to change much from 2016 to 2026. It may decrease by less than 1%, or about one hundred jobs.

---

wear the company's products. They are often shown having fun or spending time with family. They make the clothing or other products look useful, comfortable,

Some models appear on billboard advertisements.

and fashionable. Other models work in stores. They talk about how a fabric feels. They show different features of a product, such as zippers and pockets. They try to convince customers to buy the products.

Models work closely with photographers. They pose for photos. They move slightly for each photo. This shows different angles of the product. They change their facial expression. Their appearance helps create a certain look. It might be serious or playful. It might be casual or formal. Fashion companies use models to add feeling and style to their products.

A model's photos may appear in ads. This includes ads in newspapers and magazines. Models also show off fashion in store catalogs, posters, and billboards.

Some models walk on runways or stand in stores. This helps people see how fashion looks in real life. In stores, customers can ask the models questions.

Sometimes models go to trade shows. They show off products made by a company or designer. Other people may buy the products. Models can connect with other professionals at trade shows. This can help them build their careers.

A model's work schedule varies. Many models work part-time. This is because modeling jobs only employ them for a short period of time. Models may work odd hours. Sometimes they get hired for a job on short notice. Photo shoots can last several hours. Models may be asked to travel to fashion or trade shows. They

Models may try to look serious in photo shoots if they are showing off high-end or formal clothing.

may have periods of unemployment. Many people want to model. Modeling jobs are often competitive.

TRAINING

Some people go to modeling school. They learn skills such as posing, walking on

Models show off clothing and accessories, such as purses.

a runway, and applying makeup. But no education is required to become a model.

Most models apply to modeling agencies. They sign **contracts** with agencies. These agencies work with fashion companies. They help models find auditions and jobs. Fashion companies seek out models. They ask agencies who is available. Agencies promote the models they work with. They receive part of the money that their models earn.

Models should research agencies before signing a contract with them. They should find the agency that is best for them. They should make sure the agency has a good reputation. Well-known agencies can find many job opportunities for their models.

Some models do not sign with agencies. They work directly with companies.

They promote themselves. Some experienced models do this. It is difficult for new models to find work on their own.

Models audition for jobs. Companies often have height, weight, or clothing size requirements. Some companies try to find celebrity models to promote their products. Others try to find unknown or new models.

Models create portfolios. A portfolio is a collection of the work they have done. It shows photos or ads they have been in. It also shows the companies they have worked with. Models need composite cards, too. A composite card shows the

Models practice certain skills, such as how to walk on a runway.

best photos from a model's portfolio.

It lists the model's body measurements.

Models take their portfolio and composite card to auditions. Companies look at these materials when deciding whom to hire.

Tailors help adjust clothes to fit models.

Some models focus on one area of the fashion industry. They might only take jobs with certain companies. They might only model certain products, such as women's athletic clothing. Parts models only model one body part. Hand and foot models are parts models. Hand models might advertise nail polish. Foot models might promote shoes.

LOOKING AHEAD

Modeling jobs are competitive. Many people audition for one job. However, all types of models are needed. Companies look for a variety of models. They seek out models of different heights, weights, and ages. It is important for diverse models to be shown in the fashion industry. Plus-sized models show off larger clothing sizes. Tess Holliday is a well-known plus-size model. She is also an activist. She supports women's rights and body positivity. Body positivity is a movement. It spreads the idea that people should be accepting of their bodies. She said, "For so long advertising hasn't been inclusive when it comes to plus sizes which is crazy to me. Hair and makeup are things used by everyone—it doesn't make any sense."

Rebekah Marine began modeling in 2011. She models around the world and does speaking events. She is known as the bionic model. She was born without the lower part of her right arm. She has a prosthesis, or a device that replaces the

Tess Holliday is a successful model and activist.

missing part of her arm. She said, "The fashion industry is just such a huge platform for me to prove to people that you can do anything that you want to do." She shows people that body differences do not limit models in the fashion industry.

Model Rebekah Marine is well known around the world.

Models will always be needed. New job opportunities are rising online. Many companies have websites. They advertise products on social media. They need models to promote their products in new ways.

FIND OUT MORE

Backstage

website: www.backstage.com

Backstage lists modeling, theater, and film jobs available in cities around the world. It shares information about auditions.

The Better Business Bureau (BBB)

website: www.bbb.org

The BBB helps models research modeling agencies. It gives information on local people and businesses.

Models.com

website: https://models.com

Models.com is a website for modeling agencies and companies. It is also a resource for models and aspiring models. It shares news about the modeling industry.

CHAPTER THREE

ART DIRECTOR

Art directors review and approve designs. They work with a design team to develop products. Many industries need art directors. Art directors may work in the fashion, advertising, or movie industries.

WHAT THEY DO

Art directors work with creative directors. Creative directors come up with an idea for a product. Then art directors help develop

> **MINIMUM EDUCATION:** Bachelor's degree
>
> **PERSONAL QUALITIES:** Creative, artistic, organized, resourceful, a good communicator, a leader
>
> **CERTIFICATION AND LICENSING:** None required, but five years of experience recommended
>
> **WORKING CONDITIONS:** Many art directors are self-employed. Most partner with companies and work in office buildings.
>
> **SALARY:** The average salary in 2017 was $92,500 per year, or $44.47 per hour. The lowest 10 percent earned less than $51,130 per year. The highest 10 percent earned more than $170,230 per year.
>
> **NUMBER OF JOBS:** 90,300 in 2016
>
> **FUTURE JOB OUTLOOK:** The number of jobs is expected to grow 5% from 2016 to 2026, or an additional 4,900 jobs.

the product. Some art directors work for clothing companies. They make sure designs match a **brand's** style. Others work for fashion magazines. They choose

Art directors work with many people to develop products.

the images to use in a magazine. They also choose the font and other design elements. They shape the magazine's overall style and message. Still others may work in photography studios. They direct photography shoots.

Art directors have many responsibilities. They use business and management skills. They develop a budget and timeline for a project. They must be organized.

Art directors manage a team of people. This team can include artists, designers, and photographers. Art directors give these people direction. They tell the team about their ideas for designs or images. Then the team creates designs or images. Art directors review these materials. They give feedback about what to change. Or they may approve the materials. They select the images and designs to use in the final product. Art directors help create a variety of products. The product may be clothing. Or it may be a fashion magazine.

TRAINING

The minimum education needed to become an art director is a bachelor's degree. Most people who want to become an art director major in art or design. Experience in the industry helps people become art directors. Many people work in an artistic job first. They might be a graphic designer or

Some people work as fashion photographers before they become art directors.

photographer. They practice creating styles.

They learn how to work with companies.

Most people have about five years of

experience before becoming an art director.

Art directors give designers feedback to help improve products.

LOOKING AHEAD

Art directors will always be needed. They combine the business and creative aspects of the fashion industry. They help people work together on projects. The fashion industry is growing in new ways. Websites and online ads are popular. Art directors manage and help design websites that advertise products.

    Fabien Baron is a French art director. He has been called fashion's best-known art director. He has helped develop and advertise products for major companies. He said, "I think I have been successful because I know how to pair things together; I know how to take a problem, an equation, and solve it." He admitted it takes a lot

Art directors select images to help sell products.

of work. Art directors have many different responsibilities. But it can be rewarding to see the final products.

FIND OUT MORE

The Art Career Project

website: www.theartcareerproject.com

The Art Career Project is a website made to help people in creative careers. They can find jobs or take classes.

The One Club for Creativity

website: www.oneclub.org

The One Club hosts events and training for professionals who work in many industries, including fashion.

CHAPTER FOUR

MARKET RESEARCHER

Market researchers help companies make smart decisions. They work on the business side of the fashion industry. They help companies manage budgets and make pricing decisions. They research the **market**. The market is where companies and consumers meet.

MINIMUM EDUCATION: Bachelor's degree

PERSONAL QUALITIES: A problem solver, detail-oriented, a good communicator

CERTIFICATION AND LICENSING: Optional certification

WORKING CONDITIONS: Most market researchers work in office buildings.

SALARY: The average salary in 2017 was $63,230 per year, or $30.40 per hour. The lowest 10 percent earned less than $34,510 per year. The highest 10 percent earned more than $122,770 per year.

NUMBER OF JOBS: 595,400 in 2016

FUTURE JOB OUTLOOK: The number of jobs is expected to grow 23% from 2016 to 2026, or an additional 138,300 jobs.

Market researchers share their research with companies. This helps companies create business plans. A business plan is

Market researchers collect data to help companies grow and be successful.

an outline of the goals a company wants to achieve. These goals are determined by a company's budget. A business plan can also include marketing ideas or data from past years.

WHAT THEY DO

Market researchers first develop a research plan. This plan addresses problems or challenges a company may face. For example, a clothing company may design a trendy new shirt. But the company may know that other companies will make similar shirts. The company wants its shirt to stand out. It may hire a market researcher. The researcher looks at data from other companies. The researcher thinks of ways to help the company compete against other companies. In this way, the researcher can help the company become successful.

Market researchers collect data. They ask consumers for their opinions on products. They read people's comments about products online. Sometimes they **survey** consumers. One important part of collecting data is looking at competitors. That means finding other companies that make similar products. Researchers review sale prices. They keep track of fashion trends. They watch consumer spending habits.

Once researchers have all the data they need, they **analyze** it. They see what strategies work for other companies. They

Market researchers help people understand surveys and studies.

also see what strategies do not work for other companies. Then they write a report. The report shows their findings. It might include graphs about sales. It might have

Statistics is the science of collecting and studying data.

statistics about consumers. It could have

survey results. The researcher recommends

the best way for the company to advertise

its products. The company uses the researcher's report to make decisions.

TRAINING

The minimum education required to become a market researcher is a bachelor's degree. Many people major in market research. Others major in business, math, statistics, or computer science. They take classes about research methods and statistics.

Some market researchers get a master's degree. They study statistics, marketing, or business administration. This degree usually takes one to three years to complete.

Master's degrees help researchers advance in their career. They are more prepared for leadership positions.

Certification is optional. Some market researchers decide to become certified to show their skills. The Professional Researcher Certification has three requirements. Market researchers must pass an exam. They must have three or more years of market research experience. They must complete twelve hours of classes. To stay certified, they must complete twenty hours of classes every two years.

Market researchers are always needed to help people understand data.

LOOKING AHEAD

Market researchers help with sales and advertising. They gather data. Data helps companies make important decisions. It helps companies become successful.

David Santee was a market researcher for many years. He said, "There is more to market research than market research. The greatest value . . . many times is understanding the business issue that leads to the study."

Market researcher careers are growing. Companies need help finding the best ways to reach consumers. Market researchers are in demand.

FIND OUT MORE

The American Marketing Association (AMA)

website: www.ama.org

The AMA connects people who work in marketing. It shares marketing-related news in the *Journal of Marketing Research*.

CareerOneStop

website: www.careeronestop.org

CareerOneStop is a website run by the US Department of Labor. It offers information about many different career options.

The Insights Association

website: www.insightsassociation.org

The Insights Association is a community of market researchers and data specialists. The association offers classes and certification for market researchers.

CHAPTER FIVE

RETAIL SALESPERSON

Retail salespeople talk with customers. They help customers find products. Fashion companies rely on salespeople to sell their products.

WHAT THEY DO

Retail salespeople usually work in stores. They sell products to customers. These products may include clothes, jewelry,

MINIMUM EDUCATION: None

PERSONAL QUALITIES: Social, friendly, upbeat and positive, good at math

CERTIFICATION AND LICENSING: None

WORKING CONDITIONS: Most retail salespeople work in stores. They may have to work long or odd hours.

SALARY: The average salary in 2017 was $23,370 per year, or $11.24 per hour. The lowest 10 percent earned less than $8.61 per hour. The highest 10 percent earned more than $19.85 per hour.

NUMBER OF JOBS: 4,854,300 in 2016

FUTURE JOB OUTLOOK: The number of jobs is expected to grow 2% from 2016 to 2026, or an additional 92,400 jobs.

or accessories. Salespeople have many responsibilities. They might stand at the store's entrance and welcome people. They might fold clothes on the shelves.

Retail salespeople help sell people products in stores.

Salespeople learn the types of products customers are looking for. Then they recommend products.

Some retail salespeople focus on business tasks. They might prefer working with money. They process payments at the cash register. Other salespeople focus on communication tasks. This includes greeting people. They explain sales and store **policies**. They answer people's questions.

Some salespeople focus on fashion. They like to be creative. They set up displays in the store. They dress and arrange mannequins. They might model clothes while they work. They explain different fabrics or products to customers. They know details about the products. They help customers find fashions that suit their sizes and styles.

TRAINING

No education is required to be a retail salesperson. But many stores prefer that salespeople have at least a high school diploma. Salespeople do on-the-job training. This training can last a few days or a few months. In small stores, experienced salespeople may train new salespeople. Large stores may have training programs.

During training, salespeople practice customer service. They learn about the products they are selling. They learn about the company and its policies. It is important for salespeople to be trained and prepared.

Some salespeople dress and arrange mannequins.

People who come to the store will ask them questions.

Most salespeople work as part of a team. They stand for long periods of time. Many work evenings or weekends.

Some salespeople work in footwear stores. They sell people shoes.

Some work part-time. Stores can be busy during holidays. Many stores have extra salespeople during the months of November, December, and January. Consumers do more shopping at these times of the year.

Salespeople can advance to manager jobs. This usually happens after a few years. Managers have more responsibilities than salespeople. They oversee salespeople. They make salespeople's work schedules. They may choose which products to sell. Some managers work in more than one store location. They make sure the business is running smoothly. Some manager jobs require a bachelor's degree.

LOOKING AHEAD

Retail salespeople are always needed in the fashion industry. The job is not affected by the rise in online shopping. Many people still shop in stores. They need salespeople to help them buy products.

Mandi Hinrichs is a former retail salesperson. She said, "The most positive part of retail was that it . . . fostered people skills that have helped in every job I have had since."

Retail salespeople get to work with many people. Some salespeople enjoy talking with others. They prefer to be active instead of sitting at a desk. Some like to focus on business tasks. Others like to focus on fashion. This variety makes the job a good fit for many people.

FIND OUT MORE

The National Retail Federation (NRF)

website: https://nrf.com/

The NRF is a community of companies and employees in the retail industry. It educates people about the industry.

O*NET OnLine

website: www.onetonline.org

O*NET OnLine has information about different career paths. It helps people find the job that is the best fit for them.

The Retail Industry Leaders Association (RILA)

website: www.rila.org

The RILA is a group of retail company leaders who work together. The RILA makes policies to help consumers and companies. It connects people within the retail industry.

INTERVIEW WITH A PROFESSIONAL

Jim Kuerschner is the president of the fashion company KULE. KULE is located in New York City. It designs men's and women's clothing.

WHY DID YOU DECIDE TO WORK IN THE FASHION INDUSTRY?

I fell into the fashion industry by chance. Originally, I wanted to pursue a career as an entertainment attorney. But after meeting a personable retail director at a party one night, I was convinced to try a gig in fashion public relations. The principal requirement was being hyper-organized and good with people as well as having an eye for product. I turned my freelancing into a part-time job. I worked retail sales for a designer women's brand that sold, designed, and produced goods all in one building. I loved being surrounded by creative people, meeting new customers every day, and being involved with a small operation. I found I had a knack for selling . . . and knowing which products would sell.

CAN YOU DESCRIBE YOUR TYPICAL WORK DAY?

Each morning, I start by reading the latest industry news. After that, my days vary wildly, depending on the season. We produce four collections a year, so we're always selling one collection in stores and online, selling another at wholesale (to other boutiques and retail partners), and designing another. I review our website performance, craft our marketing strategy and messages, manage a team of retail employees, and make sure all of our factories get paid on time. I work closely with our sales, public relations, production, and operations teams to make sure everything is running smoothly.

WHAT DO YOU LIKE MOST ABOUT YOUR JOB?

I like having my hand in all aspects of the business, and I like that no two days are the same. I also love the mix of creative and analytical thinking that the job requires. Not only do I ensure that our finances and warehouse operations are in order, I also work with brilliant photographers to create beautiful images and talented designers to create beautiful products.

WHAT PERSONAL QUALITIES DO YOU FIND MOST VALUABLE FOR THIS TYPE OF WORK?

You need to be organized, creative, analytical, and have an eye for design. You need to be a problem solver, stay calm under pressure, and communicate your ideas clearly. Lastly, you need to enjoy selling.

WHAT ADVICE DO YOU HAVE FOR STUDENTS WHO MIGHT BE INTERESTED IN THIS CAREER?

Stay on top of trends and business news through online sources. . . . Try to find an internship or a part-time job with a fashion boutique or brand so you can get a feel for what a career in this industry would be like. Chat with people you know in the business who can give you insight into their jobs.

OTHER JOBS IN THE FASHION INDUSTRY

- Accountant
- Brand Strategist
- Buyer
- Cashier
- Dressmaker
- Editor
- Fashion Director
- Marketing Coordinator
- Marketing Manager
- Media Planner
- Merchandiser
- Photographer
- Producer
- Purchasing Manager
- Sales Inventory Analyst
- Sales Manager
- Store Manager
- Stylist
- Tailor
- Textile Machine Operator
- Trend Forecaster
- Videographer
- Web Developer

Editor's Note: The US Department of Labor's Bureau of Labor Statistics provides information about hundreds of career options. The agency's Occupational Outlook Handbook describes the education and skill requirements, pay, and future outlook for each job. The Occupational Outlook Handbook can be found online at www.bls.gov/ooh.

GLOSSARY

analyze
to study the results of a survey or test

brand
a group of products that reflect a certain style

consumer
a person who buys a product

contract
a formal agreement between two or more people

major
the main subject a student studies at a college or university

market
a place or network where people buy products

policy
a rule or guideline about what to do in certain situations

runway
a raised platform

statistic
a number, such as a percentage, that represents a piece of information

survey
to ask people to complete a poll, or a list of questions

INDEX

accessories, 12, 21, 23, 65
agencies, 32–33, 41
art directors, 4, 42–50

Baron, Fabien, 49–50
billboards, 29
blogs, 7
brands, 43
budgets, 45, 52, 54
buyers, 19

catalogs, 29
clothes, 6, 8–9, 12, 14–17, 19, 21–23, 27, 34, 36–37, 43, 46, 55, 64–65, 67
computer-aided design (CAD), 15, 20
costumes, 21, 23

designers, 4, 6, 10–11, 12–24, 25, 30, 45, 46

fabrics, 15, 19–20, 28, 67
fashion show, 6–7, 23, 26
footwear, 5, 9, 21, 23, 37
Ford, Tom, 17

Holliday, Tess, 37–38

jewelry, 12, 17, 64

magazines, 8, 29, 43–44, 46
makeup, 32, 38
mannequins, 8, 67
Marine, Rebekah, 38–39
market researchers, 52–62, 63
Miller, Nicole, 16–17
models, 6–8, 11, 12, 26–40, 41

news, 7, 11, 29, 41, 63

photography, 6–8, 11, 28–30, 34–35, 45, 47
portfolios, 20, 34–35
posters, 29

retail stores, 8, 11, 19, 26, 28, 29, 53, 64–72, 73

salespeople, 8, 11, 64–72, 73
social media, 40
style, 6, 8, 10, 12, 15, 27, 29, 43–44, 47, 67

television, 23, 26
trade shows, 19, 30
travel, 19, 30
trends, 11, 20, 55–56

IMAGE CREDITS

Cover: © Odua Images/Shutterstock Images
4–5: © Red Line Editorial
7: © Nata Sha/Shutterstock Images
9: © Kateryna Larina/Shutterstock Images
10: © Gorynvd/Shutterstock Images
14: © Nenad Aksic/Shutterstock Images
16: © Redpixel.pl/Shutterstock Images
18: © Ovidiu Hrubaru/Shutterstock Images
21: © Bambax/Shutterstock Images
22: © RossHelen/Shutterstock Images
24: © Borka Kiss/Shutterstock Images
28: © SeaRain/Shutterstock Images
31: © FashionStock.com/Shutterstock Images
32: © Dima Babushkin/Shutterstock Images
35: © Keleny/Shutterstock Images
36: © Jacob Lund/Shutterstock Images
39: © Kathy Hutchins/Shutterstock Images
40: © FashionStock.com/Shutterstock Images
44: © Rawpixel.com/Shutterstock Images
47: © studioalaska/Shutterstock Images
48: © Kzenon/Shutterstock Images
50: © Leonardo Patrizi/iStockphoto
54: © Jacob Lund/Shutterstock Images
57: © fizkes/Shutterstock Images
58: © MorePixelsShutterstock/Shutterstock Images
61: © Song_about_summer/Shutterstock Images
66: © Monkey Business Images/Shutterstock Images
69: © Creative Lab/Shutterstock Images
70: © YinYang/iStockphoto

ABOUT THE AUTHOR

Emma Huddleston lives in the Twin Cities with her husband. She enjoys writing children's books, but she likes reading novels even more. When she is not writing or reading, she likes to stay active by running and swing dancing. She thinks careers in fashion can be glamorous and practical.